aaron .

The Caring Creator

God's Love for his World

CARINE MACKENZIE

Christian Focus Publications

©1992 Christian Focus Publications
Published by
Christian Focus Publications Ltd
Geanies House, Fearn, Tain,
Ross-shire, IV20 1TW, Scotland, UK

ISBN 0 - 906731 - 05 -4

Text by Carine MacKenzie

Illustrations by Mike Taylor
Designed by Seoris N McGillivray
Typography by Hiscan, Inverness

Contents

1 THE FIRST SEVEN DAYS

HOW GOD MADE THE WORLD 5
LIGHT IS GIVEN 6
WATER EVERYWHERE 7
LAND APPEARS 9
SUN, MOON AND STARS 10
BIRDS AND FISH 12
ANIMALS AND MAN 14
DAY OF REST 16

2 SIN SPOILS THE PERFECT WORLD

HOWEVER DID IT HAPPEN? 19
SATAN TEMPTS EVE 20
GOD'S PUNISHMENT 22
GOD'S PROMISE 25

3 THE CREATOR COMES DOWN TO EARTH

HOW GOD KEPT HIS PROMISE............. 27
THE BIRTH OF THE CREATOR 28
THE LIFE OF THE CREATOR 30
THE TEACHING OF THE CREATOR ... 33
THE DEATH OF THE CREATOR 34

4 THE CREATOR'S PLAN

WHAT WILL HAPPEN NEXT 37
ALL MADE NEW 39

5 WHAT ABOUT YOU?

The Caring Creator

1 THE FIRST SEVEN DAYS

This story is found in the Bible, in Genesis chapters 1 and 2.

We live in a very wonderful world - the planet EARTH, which is a small part of the universe.

Our world, and the whole universe did not come into being by accident. It was created by God. God had no beginning. He has always existed.

God created the world and everything that is in it from nothing. God is all-powerful. He spoke a few words and the different parts of the creation came into being. He did this in six days and rested on the seventh day.

How God made
the World

Light is given

On the first day God created light. He said, "Let there be light," and the light appeared immediately. Light is necessary for all life.

God thought that the light was good. He separated it from the darkness. God called the light DAY and the darkness NIGHT.

Day and night are part of God's well-ordered world.

Water everywhere

On the second day God created the atmosphere. When we look up into the sky we see different types of clouds - some dark and full of rain, others white and fluffy. Every cloud in the sky has been made by God.

God made the seas and rivers. The water that covers more than half of the earth's surface was made by God. The water that springs up from under the earth to flow to the sea as a river was made by God. The water that forms huge lakes or little ponds was all made by God.

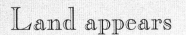

Land appears

On the third day God spoke again, and the dry land appeared out of the water. Mountains, plains and valleys were created by his power.

God said, "Let the land produce vegetation, all sorts of plants and trees." By God's power plants and trees were made. Tall trees, bushes, flowers - all producing seed so that the vegetation would reproduce and spread.

God saw that what he had made was good.

Sun, Moon and Stars

On the fourth day God made the sun, moon and stars.

"Let there be lights in the sky," he said.

"Let them be the forces which bring order to the seasons and the days and the years. Let them also give light to the world."

So God made the sun which shines during the day and the moon which shines on our world at night-time. He then made the stars which we see in the night sky.

God saw that what he had made was good.

Birds and Fish

On the fifth day God made sea-creatures and birds.

"Let the waters be filled with living beings and let birds fly across the sky," said God.

With these words he created all sorts of sea creatures - the octopus, the shark, the sea-anemone and the limpet.

God also made the birds - the majestic eagle, the duck, the sea-gull and the swan.

God blessed the sea creatures and the birds. He made them with the ability to produce young ones. He instructed them to be fruitful and increase in number.

Animals and Man

On the sixth day God made the animals.

"Let the land produce living creatures," he said.

With these words all kinds of animals came into being - lions, donkeys, cows, badgers, bats and moles.

God saw that what he had made was good. Then he came to the climax of his creative work.

"Let us make man in our own image," he said. "Man will rule over the fish in the sea and the birds in the air and over all the animals and creeping things."

So God made the first human being in his own image. The Lord God made a man from the dust of the ground. He breathed the breath of life into his nostrils and so man became a living soul.

God did not want the man called Adam to be alone so he made a woman to be a help and companion for him. He caused Adam to fall into a very deep sleep. While he was sleeping God took one of Adam's ribs then closed the flesh again. From this rib God made a woman. He gave Adam the woman, Eve, to be his wife and he was glad. "She is part of me," he said, "bone of my bone and flesh of my flesh."

God blessed Adam and Eve. He told them to be fruitful, to produce children. He told them to rule over all other living creatures. God gave them the plants and the fruits for food. Adam had the task of giving names to all the animals - this showed that he was in charge of them.

God saw that everything that he had made was very good.

Day of Rest

The great work of creation was completed in six days. On the seventh day God rested from all his work. He was not tired or weary. The world that he had made was perfect and complete. God rested to admire his work. It was all very good.

God made the seventh day special. He blessed it and made it holy. This is the day when we worship God in a special way. We thank him for his wisdom and power and love. We think about his goodness to us and all the wonderful gifts he has given us. God cares for us and for all he has made.

2 SIN SPOILS THE PERFECT WORLD

This story is found in the Bible, in Genesis chapter 3.

God's perfect world has become flawed. Weeds spoil the gardens, hard work is needed to gain a living from the land; there is ugliness, pollution and disease. Men and women today are not perfect. There is hatred and greed and fighting, vandalism and lying.

What has happened to God's perfect creation? It has been spoiled by the sin which entered the world. Men and women have sinful hearts and think evil thoughts. They say things that are wrong and do things that are bad.

How did this happen?

However did
it happen?

Satan tempts Eve

The Lord God gave Adam and Eve a magnificent garden to live in - the Garden of Eden. There were lovely trees with delicious fruit to eat. Adam was given the delightful task of looking after this beautiful garden.

"You are free to eat from any tree," said God, "except the tree of the knowledge of good and evil which is in the middle of the garden. If you eat of that tree you will surely die."

Satan the prince of evil, came to tempt Eve. He came in the form of a serpent and spoke to her. First of all he questioned God's words.

"Did God really say that you must not eat from one tree in the garden?" he asked.

"Yes," replied Eve. "We can eat from all the trees in the garden except the one in the middle. We must not touch that one or we will die."

Then Satan said that God's words were not true.

"You will not die," he said. "God knows that if you eat that fruit you will be as wise as he is, knowing good and evil."

Eve was taken in by Satan's arguments. She looked at the forbidden fruit and wanted it. She took some from the tree and ate it. She gave the fruit to Adam too and he ate it. Sin entered into the world and Adam and Eve were no longer innocent. They realised that they were naked and felt ashamed. They sewed fig leaves together to make clothes for themselves.

God's Punishment

Adam and Eve knew that they had been disobedient. They heard the sound of God walking in the garden as the day grew cooler and were afraid to meet him. Adam and Eve hid among the trees in the garden.

God called out to Adam, "Where are you?"

Adam answered,
"I heard you in the garden and I was afraid because I was naked.
So I hid."

"How do you know that you are naked?" demanded God. "Have you eaten from the tree that I have forbidden?"

Adam tried to pass on the blame.

"The woman that you put here with me is to blame. She gave me some of the fruit and I ate it."

God turned to Eve. "What have you done?" he asked.

Eve tried to make an excuse too.

"The serpent deceived me, and I ate the fruit," she claimed.

God has to punish sin. He spoke first to the serpent.

"Because of your actions, you are cursed more than any other living creature. You will crawl along the ground all your life. You will eat dust. There will be enmity between you and the woman; between your children and hers. The woman's son will crush your head and you will hurt his heel."

Eve was punished too.

"You will have pain when you give birth to a child. You will be dependant on your husband. He will rule over you."

Adam too had to bear punishment.

"You will have to work hard all your life. The ground will not be easy to manage any more. There will be thorns and thistles to make it difficult. You will produce food to eat but you will sweat with all the hard work."

Even in this punishment God showed his care. He did not cut them off completely. There was the prospect of having children and food. God also made clothes for Adam and Eve from animal skins.

God sent Adam and Eve away from the Garden of Eden for ever. They were never allowed to return.

God's Promise

Even though it was a sad and difficult time, God still showed mercy to Adam and Eve and to their children, including you. Satan wanted to destroy Adam and Eve and to spoil their relationship with God. He is very wicked and clever. But God had a better plan for the people of the world.

"The serpent and the woman's child will be enemies," said God.

Satan and the Lord Jesus Christ, the most important child ever born to any woman, will be enemies. Satan will try to hurt Jesus but Jesus will utterly defeat Satan and the power of sin. God had promised this before Adam and Eve left the Garden of Eden.

We have seen this promise fulfilled. Jesus came to earth as a man. He died on the cross to take the punishment required for sin. God's justice demanded such a sacrifice. Satan was completely defeated. God loves to show mercy to sinners who trust in the Lord Jesus Christ and what he has done.

God has shown his mercy and love to us in so many ways.

Noah was shown the rainbow to remind him and us of God's promise that he would not destroy the whole earth by flood again. (Genesis 9: 11-17)

Abraham was assured by God that he would be with him and that his descendants would be as many as the stars in the sky or the sand on the seashore. (Genesis 22: 17-18)

God spoke to Solomon after the temple was completed. He promised that he would be with him and his family if they remained faithful to God and his laws. (1 Kings 9: 4-7)

God's promise to send the Saviour has been kept.

The Caring Creator

3 THE CREATOR COMES DOWN TO EARTH

God fulfilled his promise made first in the Garden of Eden,
in a wonderful way.

"A man would have victory over Satan," God had said.

What man would be able to do that?

God loved the world so much that he sent his one and only Son. God the Son
was equal in power and glory with God the Father and God the Holy Spirit.
God the Son became a human and was born in our world in the town of
Bethlehem in Judea nearly 2,000 years ago. His name was Jesus.

How God kept his Promise

The Birth of the Creator

Jesus, the Son of God, with God the Father and God the Holy Spirit had created the whole world. Would his birthplace be the most spectacular situation, the best palace, the most important city? No! Jesus, the Creator, ws born in an unimportant little town, Bethlehem. His birthplace was not even a house but in a stable among the animals that he had made. There was no room for him anywhere. His mother Mary and her husband Joseph were poor people.

Jesus' birth was announced by the angels whom he had created. One spoke to some shepherds telling them the good news that a Saviour had been born. A large choir of angels appeared praising God.

"Glory to God in the highest and on earth peace to men on whom his favour rests," they sang.

The wise men from the east noticed a special star in the sky and followed it to Bethlehem. There they worshipped the child Jesus and gave him presents. A star that God the Son had made, led these wise men to him.

The Life of the Creator

Throughout his life the Lord Jesus showed on many occasions his power over creation.

One evening Jesus and his friends were in a boat crossing the Sea of Galilee. Suddenly a violent storm blew up on the lake; the waves washed over the boat. His friends shouted in terror,

"Lord, save us. We are going to drown!"

Jesus stood up in the boat and spoke to the wind and waves.

"Quiet! Be still!"

Jesus, God the Son, who had made the wind and water, used the power of his word to control the storm. The wind died down and all was calm.

Early one morning Jesus travelled by foot into the city of Jerusalem. He was hungry. By the side of the road was a fig tree, so Jesus went over to gather some figs to eat. The fig tree had nothing on it but leaves - no fruit at all.

"This tree will never bear fruit again," said Jesus. Immediately the tree withered. Jesus, who had made all the trees by speaking a few words, had power over this one fig tree. Others were amazed to see how quickly it had withered.

Crowds of people would come to hear Jesus preach - even out in the lonely country places. One day over 5,000 people stayed late to hear his wise words.

"They will need something to eat before they walk back home," he said.

There were no shops nearby but a young boy had a picnic of five barley loaves and two small fishes. Jesus blessed this small meal and it became enough to feed every person there. There were even twelve baskets of leftovers. Jesus had made the barley and the fish in the beginning.

Jesus had power over the animals too. A young untamed donkey, which no one had ever ridden before, was brought to him. Cloaks were placed on its back and Jesus rode on it into Jerusalem. He was going there to face his death but he rode into the city in triumph.

The Teaching of the Creator

Jesus used different parts of his creation to teach important lessons to his listeners.

The sheep that he had made were like people who followed the Lord. Sometimes one would stray from the flock, but the good shepherd would search for the lost sheep until he found it.

Jesus used the little grain of mustard seed to show what his kingdom is like. The seed is so small, yet it eventually produces a huge tree. The kingdom of Jesus may seem to have a very small beginning, yet it will grow and flourish.

Jesus said that storms and floods were like the troubles and difficulties of life. A storm and flood would cause the destruction of a house that did not have a solid foundation. If our life is not founded on the rock, Jesus Christ, then it will not stand the test of problems and trouble.

In his teaching, Jesus also warned about what will happen before the end of the world.

"There will be wars and earthquakes and famines in various places," he said.

God, who made the whole world, knows exactly what is happening to it. God is in control.

The Death of the Creator

The Lord Jesus, God the Son, was put to death on a cross at Calvary, just outside the city of Jerusalem.

Jesus, who had made all the trees, was nailed to a cross made of wood.

Jesus, who had made the water, called out in agony, "I am thirsty."

Sharp thorns, which came into the world as a result of sin, were made into a crown which dug into his head.

Jesus, the Creator, suffered and died for the sins of others. His suffering and death was to take the punishment for his own people who love and trust him.

While Jesus was suffering on the cross, from twelve noon till three o'clock in the afternoon there was darkness over the land. The sun which Jesus had made was hidden.

At the moment when Jesus died, the earth shook and the rocks split open. Some tombs broke open and bodies of holy people rose to life again and went into Jerusalem where they were seen by many people. The soldiers who were guarding the cross were terrified.

"Surely this is the Son of God," they said.

Jesus died on the cross so that his people could have everlasting life in heaven. Those who trust in him have their sins forgiven. Their lives are made new. They are called a new creation.

4 THE CREATOR'S PLAN

Many people are very afraid about what is
happening to our world. The equatorial rain
forests are being cut down and the land is left
useless. We are told that the ozone layer round
the world is changing. The sea and air and the
land are becoming polluted by chemicals.
Some animals are becoming extinct. Some
people say the world will be destroyed unless
we take better care of it.

But God still cares for us and for all
he has made.

What does God say about his world? He has a
plan for his creation. His power made it and his
power will keep it for as long as he wishes.

What will happen next ?

All made new

God tells us that the world as we know it will be destroyed one day. Everything will be destroyed by fire and the earth laid bare. Because of this we are urged to live holy and godly lives. Sinners who do not believe in Jesus will be punished. Satan will also be punished. He will not be able to spoil God's creation again.

Those who trust in the Lord Jesus have no need to be afraid of what will happen. God has promised a new heaven and a new earth. The same power which made the world will make a new one. All creatures will be made new - the wolf and the lamb will be friends: the lion will be as tame as the ox.

We cannot imagine that. With God all things are possible.

All who trust in Jesus will be there. There will be no sin to spoil God's work.

God made the world for his own glory. The whole creation is his.

5 WHAT ABOUT YOU ?

You are part of God's creation. He made you. Like everything else, you have been spoiled by sin. You need to be made new too. Your sins need to be punished but if you are sorry for your sin and ask God to forgive you, he will. Jesus Christ has taken the punishment for the sin of his people. When you trust in the Lord Jesus it is like being born again. It is the start of a new life when you serve and obey God. The same power that made the world, can make you a new creation.

We have a duty to look after the world that God has given to us. We should be kind to the animals and birds. We should do all we can to preserve the trees and plants. We should be careful not to pollute the water or the atmosphere. We have a duty to help our fellow human beings all we can. Our most important duty is to trust in the Lord Jesus and to tell others the good news of the caring Creator.

"Go into all the world and preach the good news to all creation." (Mark 16:15)